THE OFFICIAL
EVERTON FOOTBALL CLUB
ANNUAL 2017

Written by Everton Football Club
Designed by Lucy Boyd

A Grange Publication

© 2016. Published by Grange Communications Ltd., Edinburgh, under licence from Everton Football Club. Printed in the EU.

Photographs © Everton Football Club

ISBN 978-1-911287-04-9

CONTENTS

6   The Ronald Koeman Story...

8   Meet Koeman's Crew!

10 Goodison Fan Zone

12 Bomber Lives the Dream!

14 Player Profiles

16 Quiz: Against the Blues

17 Quiz: And If You Know Your History...

18 The Everton Show

20 Everton in the Community

22 If You Know Your History...

24 Quiz: The Local Lads

25 Quiz: And If You Know Your History...

26 Everton Ladies

28 The Next Generation

30 Player Profiles

32 Goodison Park Timeline

34	Quiz: Legends v The Blues	48	Predictions
36	Hat-Trick Heroes	49	Spot the Difference
38	Wordsearch	50	Euro 2016 Round-Up
39	Quiz: Test a Grown-Up!	52	Penalty Shoot-Out
40	Player Profiles	54	Everton Supporters' Clubs
42	Quiz: International Dozen...	56	My Year... Leighton Baines
44	evertontv	58	Everton Victorious!
45	evertonfc.com	60	Quiz Answers
46	Player Profiles		

THE RONALD KOEMAN STORY...

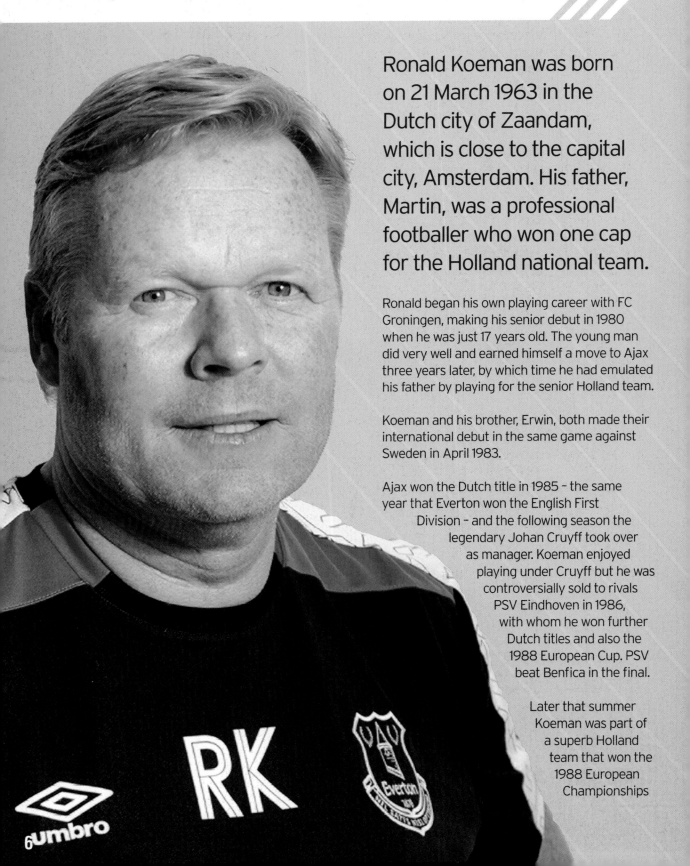

Ronald Koeman was born on 21 March 1963 in the Dutch city of Zaandam, which is close to the capital city, Amsterdam. His father, Martin, was a professional footballer who won one cap for the Holland national team.

Ronald began his own playing career with FC Groningen, making his senior debut in 1980 when he was just 17 years old. The young man did very well and earned himself a move to Ajax three years later, by which time he had emulated his father by playing for the senior Holland team.

Koeman and his brother, Erwin, both made their international debut in the same game against Sweden in April 1983.

Ajax won the Dutch title in 1985 - the same year that Everton won the English First Division - and the following season the legendary Johan Cruyff took over as manager. Koeman enjoyed playing under Cruyff but he was controversially sold to rivals PSV Eindhoven in 1986, with whom he won further Dutch titles and also the 1988 European Cup. PSV beat Benfica in the final.

Later that summer Koeman was part of a superb Holland team that won the 1988 European Championships in Germany alongside the likes of Ruud Gullit and Marco van Basten. Koeman was named in the Team of the Tournament.

He was by now a defender with an excellent worldwide reputation and in 1989 he teamed up again with Johan Cruyff who was the coach of Barcelona. More success followed for the Dutchmen. Alongside teammate Pep Guardiola, Koeman helped Barca win four successive La Liga championships from 1991-1994. The team also won their first ever European Cup final in 1992.

Barcelona beat Sampdoria (Italy) in the final 1-0 with Koeman scoring the goal.

Whilst at the Nou Camp, Koeman was Barcelona's regular penalty-taker and once went on a run of scoring from 25 consecutive spot-kicks!

After six trophy-packed seasons in Spain, Koeman returned to Holland in 1995 to join Feyenoord – becoming one of very few players to have played for the Dutch 'big three' of Ajax, PSV and Feyenoord. During his time there he played at Goodison Park where he was part of the team that knocked Everton out of the European Cup Winners' Cup!

After hanging up his boots, Koeman's first coaching job was as the assistant manager of Holland, a position he also occupied with Barcelona.

But he was always determined to be a manager in his own right and, after a spell at Vitesse Arnhem, he was appointed as the head coach of Ajax in 2001. He left there in 2005 to manage Portuguese giants Benfica but after just one season at the Stadium of Light he returned to Holland to take over at PSV, where he won the 2007 Dutch League.

From PSV, Koeman headed to Spain to coach Valencia and then back to his homeland with AZ Alkmaar and Feyenoord. The last appointment made him the first man to play for and manage the 'big three' in Holland.

In 2014, Ronald Koeman became a Premier League manager when he replaced Mauricio Pochettino at Southampton. Whilst at St Mary's he led Southampton to seventh and sixth placed finishes in the table and also won the Premier League Manager of the Month on three occasions.

It was this sort of form that prompted the Everton Board of Directors to appoint him as the manager at Goodison Park in June 2016.

RONALD KOEMAN'S HONOURS

AS A PLAYER

AJAX
- Eredivisie (Dutch League): 1984-85
- KNVB Cup (Dutch Cup): 1985-86

PSV EINDHOVEN
- Eredivisie: 1986-87, 1987-88, 1988-89
- KNVB Cup (Dutch Cup): 1987-88, 1988-89
- European Cup: 1987-88
- Dutch Footballer of the Year: 1987, 1988

BARCELONA
- La Liga (Spanish League): 1990-91, 1991-92, 1992-93, 1993-94
- Copa del Rey (Spanish Cup): 1989-90
- European Cup: 1991-92
- UEFA Super Cup: 1992
- UEFA Champions League top scorer: 1993-94

HOLLAND
- UEFA European Championship: 1988
- UEFA European Championship 1988 Team of the Tournament

AS A MANAGER

AJAX
- Eredivisie: 2001-02, 2003-04
- KNVB Cup (Dutch Cup): 2001-02
- Johan Cruyff Shield: 2002

PSV EINDHOVEN
- Eredivisie: 2006-07

VALENCIA
- Copa del Rey (Spanish Cup): 2007-08

MEET KOEMAN'S CREW!

Get to know more about the Everton manager's backroom team with this list of fun facts!

ERWIN KOEMAN
ASSISTANT MANAGER

- Erwin followed in his father Martin's footsteps by playing for Dutch side Groningen. In fact, all three Koemans (Ronald as well!) played for them **AND** one of the sides of Groningen's Euroborg stadium is named the Koeman Stand!
- He has a son, Len, who is a youth player for Helmond Sport in Holland's second division.
- Like his younger brother Ronald, Erwin was part of the Holland team that won the European Championships in 1988 and he also played at the 1990 World Cup in Italy.
- He was a manager in his own right before working with his brother. Indeed, Erwin has coached Dutch sides RKV Waalwijk, Feyenoord, Utrecht and Eindhoven and had a two-year stint in charge of the Hungarian national team!
- The brothers faced each other in the dugout as managers across two seasons when Erwin was at Waalwijk and Ronald at Feyenoord.
- Erwin claims that the best game he has ever watched is when Ronald scored the winner for Barcelona in the European Cup final against Sampdoria at Wembley in 1992.
- When asked who would play him in a movie, Erwin suggested 'Mr Bean', aka Rowan Atkinson!

JAN KLUITENBERG
FITNESS COACH

- Jan has a reputation of being a tough taskmaster!
- He has worked with Ronald Koeman rather a lot... the pair have been together at Vitesse Arnhem, Benfica, AZ Alkmaar, Feyenoord **AND** Southampton!
- Jan hasn't always been a fitness coach. When injury forced him to retire as a player early, he initially became a referee! Then, when he first went to Vitesse Arnhem, he was operations manager – which meant he was in charge of the stadium and training ground, not the players!

PATRICK LODEWIJKS
GOALKEEPING COACH

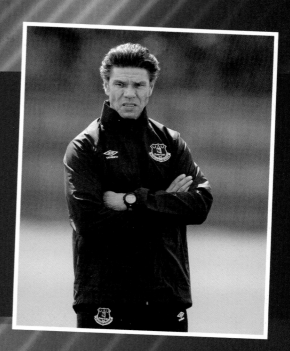

- Patrick is a bit of a legend at his old club Feyenoord. Before he arrived at Everton, he had been at the Dutch club for **FOURTEEN YEARS**!
- He ended his playing career at Feyenoord's De Kuip stadium and then immediately became a coach.
- He knows Ronald and Erwin Koeman very well – he played with them both! He shared a dressing room with Ronald at PSV Eindhoven and Erwin at Groningen.
- Patrick once got into a little argument with a referee over a penalty – with the ref sticking his tongue out at him in reply!

DAVID UNSWORTH
UNDER-23S COACH

- Unsy earned the nickname 'Rhino' during his playing career at Everton, because of his gutsy playing style and physique!
- One of his former clubs is Aston Villa. Except he never actually played a game for them because, a month after signing, Everton came calling to take him home!
- Unsy was named caretaker manager after the departure of Roberto Martinez – and boasts a 100% success rate as Everton manager!
- He has been in charge of our Under-23s since Alan Stubbs left for Hibernian in the summer of 2014.

DUNCAN FERGUSON
ASSISTANT COACH

- For a hobby, Duncan Ferguson once kept pigeons!
- In his final game for Everton, a 2-2 draw with West Brom, Big Dunc was made captain – and scored with pretty much his last ever kick!
- The popular Scotsman has worked his way up the coaching ladder at Finch Farm, having started out in October 2011 helping Kevin Sheedy with the Under-18s!

9

MATCHDAY?
IT'S SO MUCH MORE THAN JUST THE 90 MINUTES!

We all know there's nothing better than going to a live game at Goodison Park! But did you know there is so much more to see and do before you watch the Blues in action on the pitch? Let us explain more...

FANZONE

Let's start at the FanZone, the liveliest place to go before you watch the Blues! Legends such as Ian Snodin and Graham Stuart are here a lot, giving their predictions for the game ahead – and there are plenty of other special guests too!

There's live music from local bands to enjoy in the build-up to kick-off, plus plenty of chances to get involved and get up on stage yourself! You can even get your messages on the big screen and take part in competitions for prizes that cannot be won or bought anywhere else!

MATCHDAY HUB

Our newest pre-match area, the Matchday Hub is the place to be for younger Toffees.

Head down to Everton Free School on Spellow Lane before a game for free coaching sessions courtesy of Everton in the Community, facepainting, loads of food and drink, as well as our regular Match Attax station.

Also keep an eye out for some special guests, with new signings and other first-team players often heading down to meet fans!

ST LUKE'S CHURCH

And if you know your history... it's enough to make your heart go wo-oooah! You've sung the song, so now it's time to really learn about Everton's rich and glorious past!

Having lifted nine league titles, five FA Cups and a European Cup Winners' Cup, the Toffees are the fourth most successful club in the whole country.

Regularly open until 30 minutes before kick-off, the famous church on Goodison Road – the only one on the corner of a football stadium in the whole of England – is home to amazing Everton memorabilia, stories and exhibitions! And there's even a cup of tea going for mum, dad, grandad or whoever you bring along!

BOMBER LIVES THE DREAM!

In May 2016, Goodison Park staged its own piece of Merseyside sporting history.

For one night only, one of the most famous footy grounds in the country was transformed into a boxing theatre for the greatest occasion of Tony Bellew's life! A massive ring was erected just by the half-way line and thousands of seats were placed on the pitch. The Gwladys Street stand was full and the atmosphere was electric.

Lifelong Evertonian Bellew, known by all his fans as 'Bomber', had fought at Goodison before... but only in the movies! This time it was for real. As 'Pretty' Ricky Conlan, Bellew starred in the Hollywood movie 'Creed' alongside Sylvester Stallone and the climax of the film saw his character win a world title fight at Goodison Park.

It had long been Bellew's dream to do exactly the same thing in real life and that dream came true on that glorious, warm summer night.

Ilunga Makabu, from the Democratic Republic of Congo, was his opponent for the vacant WBC Cruiserweight title and around 15,000 fight fans packed Goodison Park for a night they'll never forget.

Bellew used the home dressing room at Goodison; he was dressed in blue and white for the fight and he even walked up the tunnel and out onto the pitch to the familiar sound of Z-Cars... just like the first-team players do in the Premier League. The stage was set... but it almost went horribly wrong.

FACTFILE

Full Name: Anthony Bellew
Nickname: Bomber
Date of Birth: 30 November 1982
Height: 6' 2.5"
Reach: 74 inches
First professional fight: 6 October 2007 – beat Jamie Ambler in Nottingham in the 2nd round.

Titles won:
- British Light-Heavyweight Title
- Commonwealth Light-Heavyweight Title
- WBC Silver International Light-Heavyweight Title
- WBC Silver Light-Heavyweight Title
- WBO International Cruiserweight Title
- European Cruiserweight Title
- WBC Cruiserweight World Champion

Bellew, challenging for a world title for a third time, was floored by a left hand in the very first round. However, he recovered to stop Makabu in the third round with some devastating punches that made the Wavertree-born boxer the Champion of the World.

He was delighted after the referee stopped the contest.

"I told you I am Everton," he roared from inside the ring. "That's why I got up after being knocked down in the first round. Nothing was going to stop me tonight. King Kong and 25 men wouldn't have stopped me at Goodison Park. The fans were so loud – they got me up off that floor. I achieved the dream; I am World Champion... at Goodison Park! I'm so happy. This place has been my life since I was a kid. This is the place where I come and feel so happy. I love it here."

TONY'S QUICK QUIZ

"I won the world title at Goodison Park, but here are the names of some other football stadiums in this country. See if you can tell me which team plays at each stadium... but be careful, they are not all in the Premier League! Good Luck!"

1) Britannia Stadium
2) Liberty Stadium
3) Portman Road
4) The Valley
5) Dean Court
6) Fratton Park
7) Turf Moor
8) The Riverside

Answers on p.60-61

JOEL ROBLES

BORN: 17 JUNE, 1990
PLACE OF BIRTH: MADRID, SPAIN

Joel is now in his fourth season at Everton after joining back in the summer of 2013. He signed from Atletico Madrid where he was once a teammate of Manchester United and Spain goalkeeper David de Gea. He only played seven games for Atletico and twice went out on loan - to Rayo Vallecano and Wigan Athletic where he won the FA Cup in 2012/13. Joel had to wait patiently for regular football at Goodison but he got his rewards with an extended run in the team during the second half of last season.

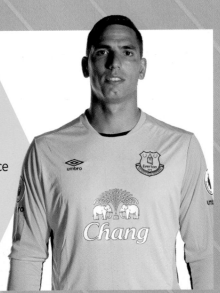

MAARTEN STEKELENBURG

BORN: 22 SEPTEMBER, 1982
PLACE OF BIRTH: HAARLEM, HOLLAND

Giant keeper Maarten was Ronald Koeman's first signing as Everton manager. The Dutchman joined from Fulham in July 2016, signing a three-year contract with the Toffees. Stekelenburg, who has also played for Ajax, Monaco and Southampton was recommended to join the Blues by his good friend Johnny Heitinga. The goalie played over 50 times for Holland, including an appearance in the 2010 World Cup final against Spain.

LEIGHTON BAINES

BORN: 11 DECEMBER, 1984
PLACE OF BIRTH: KIRKBY, ENGLAND

Leighton is one of the most experienced players in Everton's first-team squad. The left-back signed for the Toffees in the summer of 2007 and is now playing his 10th season at the football club. As a boy, he was part of Everton's Academy before moving to Wigan Athletic and then returning for £5million when he was 22 years old. The penalty and free-kick expert has now scored over 30 goals for Everton.

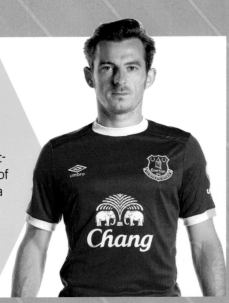

DARRON GIBSON

BORN: 25 OCTOBER, 1987
PLACE OF BIRTH: DERRY, NORTHERN IRELAND

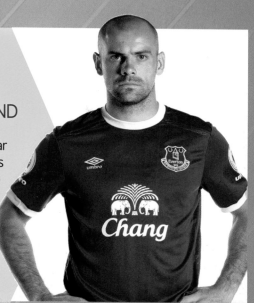

Darron extended his stay with Everton by signing a new two-year contract last summer. The central midfielder arrived at the Blues from Manchester United where he had risen to Premier League stardom through their renowned academy. Much of Gibson's time at Everton so far has been hampered by injury but he is looking to the future under Ronald Koeman's tutelage. "It's a great club, there are great people here and the dressing room is great, so I was never signing anywhere else," said Gibson after putting pen to paper on his new deal.

ASHLEY WILLIAMS

BORN: 23 AUGUST, 1984
PLACE OF BIRTH: WOLVERHAMPTON, ENGLAND

After being released from West Bromwich Albion as a teenager, Williams played for non-league Hednesford Town before turning professional at Stockport County in 2003. In 2008 he joined Swansea City and helped them win promotion to the Premier League and led them to victory in the 2013 League Cup Final. He has won over 60 caps for Wales, captaining The Dragons when they made it all the way to the Euro 2016 semi-final, losing 2-0 to eventual winners Portugal. Williams signed for Everton in the summer of 2016.

PHIL JAGIELKA

BORN: 17 AUGUST, 1982
PLACE OF BIRTH: SALE, ENGLAND

The 2016/17 season will see Phil offer a decade's worth of service to Everton's first-team. He joined the Toffees in the summer of 2007 from Sheffield United in a deal worth £4million. One of the most experienced central defenders in the Premier League, Jags has played well over 300 games for the Blues. The central defender took on the role of Club captain in the summer of 2013, following Phil Neville's retirement.

QUIZ:
AGAINST THE BLUES

See if you can recognise these seven Everton stars in action AGAINST The Blues! You get one point for knowing the player and a bonus point for knowing which team is he is playing for in the photograph...

1

2

3

4

5

6

7

Answers on p.60-61

QUIZ: AND IF YOU KNOW YOUR HISTORY...

Here are six 'matches' between current and former Everton players. All you have to do is guess who the players are and then tick the box for who played the most Premier League games for Everton!

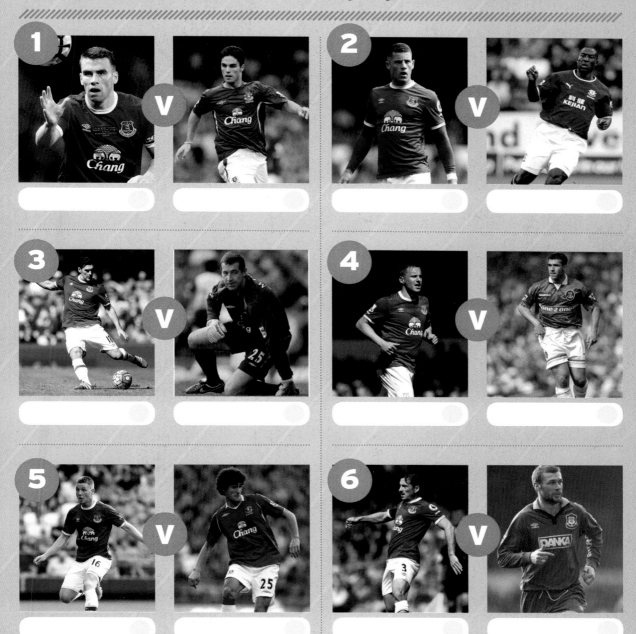

Answers on p.60-61

THE EVERTON SHOW

During the 2015/16 season,
Everton Football Club launched
our very own television show.

Called, simply, The Everton Show, the programme is filmed at a studio in south Liverpool and is aired on Bay TV each and every Friday evening.

The regular presenter is Darren Griffiths and he is joined each week by either Graham Stuart or Ian Snodin.

The show is in four segments. Part One is usually a reflection on the previous game; Part Two gets under the skin of the club with a look at the Under-21s, the Academy and the Community; Part Three is always a big sit-down interview with a current or former player and Part Four looks ahead to the next match.

"It's a simple formula but it works really well and we are very pleased at the positive reaction from the fans," said Darren.

The Everton Show has also featured some special guests on the sofa. Phil Jagielka, Leighton Baines, Kevin Sheedy and Tony Bellew have all joined Darren in the studio.

"Everyone at the club has been really supportive of the show and it's been great," added Darren. "Tony

Bellew was a terrific guest and he went out of his way to come in with the World Championship belt he had won at Goodison just a few days earlier."

After the show has been broadcast on the Friday night and then repeated on Saturday morning, it is loaded onto evertontv and YouTube so that supporters all over the world can enjoy it.

"Not only has the feedback been very good but the viewing figures are excellent as well," Darren pointed out. "A lot of hard work goes into putting the programme together and we are very proud of it. I script and present it and my colleague Matthew Gamble is the on-set producer so it's very much an in-house thing."

IT'S A SIMPLE FORMULA BUT IT WORKS REALLY WELL AND WE ARE VERY PLEASED AT THE POSITIVE REACTION FROM THE FANS

EVERTON IN THE COMMUNITY

Everton Football Club has its own official charity called Everton in the Community that helps thousands of people from all over Merseyside every year.

For over 28 years, the charity has been helping people – young and old, from many different backgrounds – in lots of ways including health, education and helping people into employment.

Everton in the Community works with children and adults to teach them about the benefits of eating healthily and doing regular exercise and also helps people find new jobs and gain qualifications.

For example, a few nights a week, the charity runs a programme called 'Kicks' all over Liverpool which gives young people a safe place to play sports and keep them off the streets and out of trouble. Also, the 'Safe Hands' programme helps young adults who have been in trouble with the police get their lives back on track.

Many of the programmes that Everton in the Community deliver are funded by the Premier League and one of these is called Premier League 4 Sport and gives school children the opportunity

Throughout the season, the players visit lots of Everton in the Community programmes to find out more about the great work they do and to meet the people that the charity helps. Sometimes they get involved with classroom or sports sessions with children and other times they spend time playing games with old people or presenting trophies to players at the charity's annual Disability Awards Ceremony.

At Christmas time, the full team visit sick children at Alder Hey Children's Hospital and deliver presents to help put smiles on the faces of the young patients and their families.

Everton in the Community also has a number of high-profile ambassadors and patrons who work to raise awareness of the charity's work, including Britain's Got Talent judge Amanda Holden and award-winning actress Dame Judi Dench.

to try sports that were popular in the London 2012 Olympics including judo, table tennis and hockey.

The charity doesn't just help children and teenagers; it helps ex-soldiers and young men who struggle with mental health problems and one of its newer programmes 'Stand Together' helps older people who are experiencing loneliness.

Everton even has its own Free School which is open to young people aged 14-19 and provides exciting learning opportunities in a fantastic new building which is just a stone's throw from Goodison Park.

The charity also fundraises throughout the year to raise money to help them continue their impressive work and there are lots of different ways that fans can get involved to help. Some fans have done a skydive, abseiled down Liverpool Cathedral and slept out at Goodison Park, whilst local schools have held sponsored silences and cake stalls to help the charity of their favourite club.

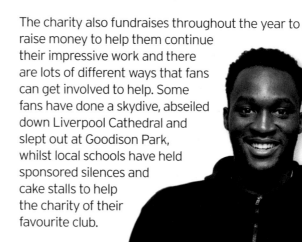

  Everton in the Community

There are lots of ways to get involved! For more details, visit
www.evertonfc.com/community

21

IF YOU KNOW YOUR HISTORY...

2017 marks the 30th anniversary of the last time that Everton won the First Division title.

In 1986, the Blues suffered the agony of losing out to Liverpool in both the Championship and the FA Cup final and so Howard Kendall was determined to put things right for the 1986/87 campaign.

However, he wasn't helped by the departure of leading goalscorer Gary Lineker to Barcelona. Lineker had top-scored in the 1986 World Cup in Mexico and the Spanish giants made Everton an offer they couldn't refuse.

Kendall also had some injury problems. For the first game of the season, against Nottingham Forest, the manager was without several key players.

Neville Southall, Footballer of the Year two years earlier, was injured and didn't play until the end of October. The Players' Player of the Year in 1985, Peter Reid, was also injured and didn't play until February. So was Pat Van Den Hauwe, who returned in February. Derek Mountfield was injured – he started just 12 games all season. Gary Stevens was missing and he didn't return until December.

It was a horrendous injury list but Kendall overcame it, signing players for modest fees who fitted in superbly well and reshuffling his squad to great effect.

Kevin Langley came from Wigan Athletic and played enough games to win a Championship medal and Alan Harper, a bit-part player two years earlier when Everton had won the 1985 title, was a regular this time around. But the jewel in Kendall's crown was a 32 year old full-back called Paul Power.

Power had played more than 400 games for Manchester City and never won anything. He came to Everton on a free transfer as cover for Pat Van Den Hauwe and promptly played in most of the games to gain himself a Championship medal.

In January, Kendall strengthened his squad for the run-in by buying Ian Snodin from Leeds United. Snodin is still at the club to this day as an official ambassador.

Without Lineker's goals, the burden of finding the back of the net was shared. Kevin Sheedy, Adrian Heath, Graeme Sharp, Paul Wilkinson and Trevor Steven all hit double figures.

The title was clinched on 4th May 1987 with a 1-0 victory at Norwich City. It was just about the furthest away trip for Everton that season but nobody was complaining as it was one long party from Norwich to Merseyside!

Everton finished nine points ahead of Liverpool – it was a remarkable title triumph achieved against all odds.

ELSEWHERE IN 1986/87

In only their tenth season as a Football League club, **Wimbledon** finished an incredible sixth in the top-flight, just behind Norwich City. The current Premier League champions, **Leicester City,** were relegated to the Second Division in 1986/87 along with **Aston Villa** and... **Manchester City**!

After a great start to the season, **Manchester United** trailed off and sacked their manager, Ron Atkinson. He was replaced by the Aberdeen boss Alex Ferguson... and we all know what happened next!

In the old Fourth Division (now League Two), **Burnley**, who are in the Premier League this season, only avoided relegation from the Football League to the Conference by one single point!

In the FA Cup, **Everton** were beaten in the fifth round by **Wimbledon** – it was the first time in four years that the Toffees hadn't reached the final. The eventual Cup winners were **Coventry City** who won it for the first time in their history by beating **Tottenham Hotspur** 3-2 in the final.

QUIZ: THE LOCAL LADS

1 Which of these former Everton players did not come through the Club's Academy?

A) Tony Hibbert

B) Leon Osman

C) Wayne Rooney

D) Dan Gosling

2 Tony Hibbert scored his only Everton goal - a stunning free-kick - in his testimonial back in 2012. Who were the opponents that day?

3 True or false: Everton's Academy produced England's leading all-time goalscorer.

4 Southport-born Jack Rodwell made 110 appearances for Everton after coming through the Academy. Which North West club did he join after leaving Goodison Park?

A) Blackburn Rovers

B) Burnley

C) Manchester United

D) Manchester City

5 The Premier League's youngest ever goalscorer is an Everton Academy graduate. Who is it?

A) Victor Anichebe

B) Kieran Dowell

C) James Vaughan

D) Ross Barkley

6 Kieran Dowell made his first-team debut against which team in the Europa League in 2014?

A) FC BATE Borisov

B) FC Krasnodar

C) OSC Lille

D) VfL Wolfsburg

AND IF YOU KNOW YOUR HISTORY...

1 Who is Everton's all-time top goalscorer?

A) Graeme Sharp

B) Bob Latchford

C) Dixie Dean

D) Joe Royle

2 How many league titles have Everton won?

A) Three

B) Five

C) Seven

D) Nine

3 Name the Everton captain who lifted the FA Cup for the Blues in 1995.

A) Phil Jagielka

B) Phil Neville

C) Kevin Ratcliffe

D) Dave Watson

4 True or false: Anfield was once the home ground of Everton.

5 BBC Match of the Day presenter Gary Lineker had one season at Everton in 1985/86. How many goals did he score that season?

A) 30

B) 35

C) 40

D) 45

6 Who won the League with Everton as a player and as a manager?

A) Joe Royle

B) Howard Kendall

C) Colin Harvey

D) Alan Ball

Answers on p.60-61

GIRLS... DO YOU WANT TO BE A FOOTBALLER? OF COURSE YOU DO!

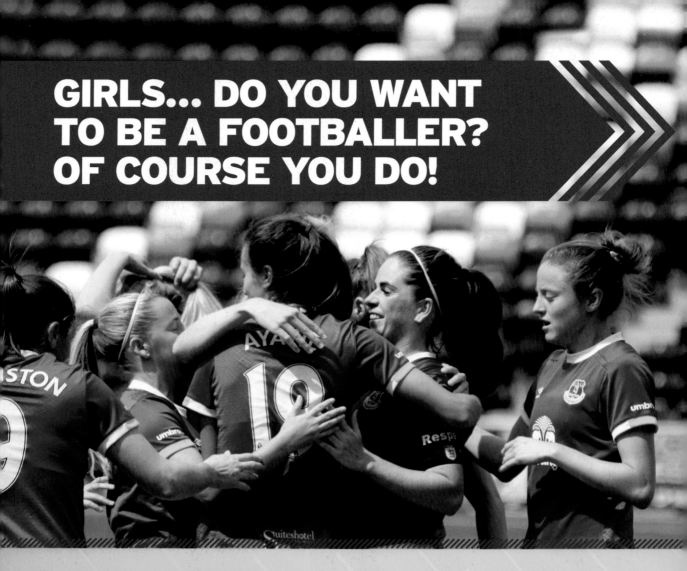

Well, we quizzed Everton Ladies captain Michelle Hinnigan to get some tips on how to make it as a Blue!

PRACTICE, PRACTICE, PRACTICE!
This is the only way to learn new skills. We work on things every day in training but when I was young, I would always play with my younger sister and cause the neighbours loads of hassle by kicking balls into their gardens, or playing football tennis over the washing line! So make sure you get out with your friends and practise as much as you can. Practise makes Perfect!

SMILE!
Make sure you always play and train with a smile on your face. I always train and play better when I smile so make sure you enjoy every minute of training and the games - one day you will look back and realise they were the best days of your life.

EAT RIGHT
Make sure your diet is the best it can be but allow yourself at least a treat a week. To get the best out of your performance, it is important to eat the correct foods to fuel yourself. You only get one body so make sure you look after it. I usually allow myself a treat meal after a game on a Sunday!

WORK HARD AND DO YOUR BEST
Day in and day out, make sure you are working as hard as you can to be the best you can be, even if that means staying after sessions to work on your weaknesses. It will not go unnoticed!

Remember - hard work beats talent when talent doesn't work hard! Always want to strive to be the best at everything you do.

LISTEN TO YOUR COACHES
Always listen to the advice from your coaches and managers. They are there to make you and

your teammates better. Trust what they say and always take any advice from them on board.

TRUST YOUR TEAMMATES
At the end of the day your teammates will be the ones battling with you on the pitch. Make sure you speak to and build good relationships with every player as you will spend most of your time with them. One thing I have learnt throughout my career is a good team spirit will win you games.

BELIEVE IN YOURSELF
Always believe in yourself and tell yourself you are good enough. You will hear it from your friends and family but you need to hear it from yourself. If you train hard and prepare right then your confidence will come with that.

WATCH PLAYERS IN YOUR POSITION
It is good to keep your knowledge and football brain ticking over. I shouldn't admit this being a Blue, but when I was young I loved watching the likes of Steven Gerrard and Paul Scholes!

I used to try to play the way they did and saw them both as role models when I was growing up. When I was younger, female footballers were not as recognised as the men but with the growth of the women's game, younger generations will have plenty of female footballers to look up to.

DISAPPOINTMENTS ARE A PART OF THE GAME
Hopefully there will be a lot of 'ups' in your career but there will also probably be a few 'downs' along the way. One of the hardest things in my football career was relegation with Everton. But always look at disappointments as learning curves and inspiration to do your best next time.

ENJOY YOUR SUCCESSES
They will pass you by quickly! I have won gold at the 2009 European Championships, the FA Cup and the World University games and when I look back I think they all went too quickly. When you have something to celebrate, do it with your friends and family. You will deserve it after all the hard work you have put in.

THE NEXT GENERATION

Everton's Academy has produced some big names in football. But who could be the next Wayne Rooney or Ross Barkley? Here are some of the Blues youngsters ready to stake their claim...

KIERAN DOWELL

DATE OF BIRTH: 10 October 1997
PLACE OF BIRTH: Osmkirk, 7.8 miles from Goodison Park
POSITION: Midfielder
EVERTON DEBUT: 11 December 2014 v FK Krasnodar (Europa League)

Kieran used to sit in the Main Stand at Goodison to cheer on the Blues. He became the 11th youngest player in our history to make a senior appearance when he came off the bench against FK Krasnodar aged just 17 years and 62 days. He scored 11 goals for the Under-21s in 2015/16 despite missing half the season through injury.

CALLUM CONNOLLY

DATE OF BIRTH: 23 September 1997
PLACE OF BIRTH: Litherland, 3.3 miles from Goodison Park
POSITION: Defender/Midfielder
EVERTON DEBUT: 16 April 2016 v Southampton (Premier League)

Callum spent time on loan at Barnsley in 2015/16. Before signing for the Toffees, he used to sit in the Upper Gwladys. He was scouted at the age of nine and has been a Blues player ever since!

MATTHEW PENNINGTON

DATE OF BIRTH: 6 October 1994
PLACE OF BIRTH: Warrington, 19.6 miles from Goodison Park
POSITION: Defender
EVERTON DEBUT: 26 August 2015 v Barnsley (Capital One Cup)

Matty has enjoyed successful loan spells with Tranmere Rovers, Coventry City and Walsall. He was named Coventry's Young Player of the Season in 2014/15 despite only playing 25 games. He's a bit of a brainbox - achieving 10 A*s in his GCSEs and two As at A-Level.

JONJOE KENNY

DATE OF BIRTH: 15 March 1997
PLACE OF BIRTH: Kirkdale, 1.2 miles from Goodison Park
POSITION: Defender
EVERTON DEBUT: 15 May 2016 v Norwich City (Premier League)

Jonjoe captained the Everton Under-21s throughout 2014/15. He scored the winning penalty as England Under-17s were crowned European champions in 2014. Before his Blues debut, Jonjoe spent time out on loan at Wigan Athletic and Oxford United.

TOM DAVIES

DATE OF BIRTH: 30 June 1998
PLACE OF BIRTH: West Derby, 3.6 miles from Goodison Park
POSITION: Midfielder
EVERTON DEBUT: 16 April 2016 v Southampton (Premier League)

Tom is the nephew of Alan Whittle, who won the league title with Everton in 1969/70. He trained with the England first team in October 2015. Tom captained England Under-17s at the 2015 World Cup in Chile.

LIAM WALSH

DATE OF BIRTH: 15 September, 1997
PLACE OF BIRTH: Huyton, England

Liam Walsh isn't the tallest of players but he has all the attributes to reach the very top. He loves a tackle, can pass and shoot and, although he hadn't played for the Everton First Team at the start of this season, he still had some Football League experience under his belt. He spent half of the previous season at League Two Yeovil Town, for who he earned some rave reviews. Born in Huyton, Liam has been capped by England at several youth levels..

JOE WILLIAMS

DATE OF BIRTH: 8 December 1996
PLACE OF BIRTH: Huyton, 7.8 miles from Goodison Park
POSITION: Midfielder
EVERTON DEBUT: N/A

Joe was named Under-21s Player of the Year in 2015/16. He was skipper of the Under-21s throughout last season. Joe won his first international cap in January 2016 for England Under-20s against Canada.

IDRISSA GUEYE

BORN: 26 SEPTEMBER, 1989
PLACE OF BIRTH: DAKAR, SENEGAL

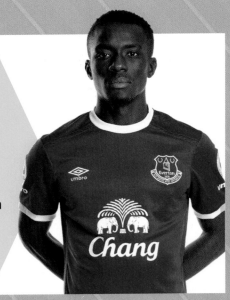

Gueye is an all-action holding midfielder who joined Everton from Aston Villa in 2016. He was born in Dakar, Senegal, and arrived in Europe with French club Lille in 2008 at the age of 17. He stayed with Lille for seven years and played against Everton in the Europa League in 2014. At the start of the 2014/15 season Gueye signed for Aston Villa and was their stand-out performer in a dreadful season for the team. He is a full Senegal international and played for them at the 2012 Olympics in London.

BRYAN OVIEDO

BORN: 18 FEBRUARY, 1990
PLACE OF BIRTH: SAN JOSE, COSTA RICA

Everton secured the signing of Costa Rica international Bryan on deadline day in August 2012. Oviedo, a versatile left-sided player who is comfortable playing both in defence and midfield, joined from Danish side FC Copenhagen for an undisclosed fee. He signed a four-year contract at Everton, a deal which has since been extended to the summer of 2019. When Bryan made his international debut for Costa Rica in 2010 against Argentina; the opposition manager was...Diego Maradona!

ROMELU LUKAKU

BORN: 13 MAY, 1993
PLACE OF BIRTH: ANTWERP, BELGIUM

The 2015/16 season saw Romelu break some goalscoring records at Everton. The £28million striker, who joined permanently in July 2014, became the Blues' highest ever scorer in a single Premier League season. His 18 goals were more than the totals previously set by Tony Cottee (in 1993/94) and Andrei Kanchelskis (in 1995/96). Earlier in the campaign, Lukaku had ended 2015 having netted 31 Club goals – the highest total in a calendar year since Bob Latchford amassed three more in 1977. He finished 2015/16 with a total of 25 goals in all competitions, meaning his average over the course of his first three seasons at Goodison was almost one every two games – impressive!

KEVIN MIRALLAS

BORN: 5 OCTOBER, 1987
PLACE OF BIRTH: LIEGE, BELGIUM

Forward, Kevin, has been at Everton for four seasons after arriving from Greek outfit Olympiakos in 2012. He has scored some great goals in his time with the Toffees, including an acrobatic volley in last season's 3-3 draw at Chelsea. Another great strike was a skilful dribble from halfway against Stoke City which won him the Goal of the Season award in the 2012/13 season. The Belgium international has also played Standard Liege and St Etienne but he missed out on a place in the Euro 2016 squad.

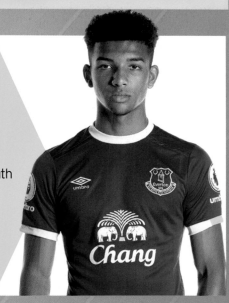

AARON LENNON

BORN: 16 APRIL, 1987
PLACE OF BIRTH: LEEDS, ENGLAND

Aaron returned for a second spell at Everton on the final day of the 2015 summer transfer window. The winger rejoined the Blues from Tottenham Hotspur on a permanent deal, following his successful loan spell with the Toffees in the second half of the 2014/15 campaign. Last season he scored six goals, including a brilliant volley against his former team Spurs and a wonderful breakaway strike at Stoke City. Aaron started his career at Leeds United and has won 21 caps for England. He was a member of the squad that travelled to South Africa for the 2010 World Cup.

MASON HOLGATE

BORN: 22 OCTOBER, 1996
PLACE OF BIRTH: DONCASTER, ENGLAND

Holgate was born in Doncaster in 1996 and joined Barnsley when he was just nine years old. He progressed through the youth ranks at Oakwell and made his debut for the first team in 2014 when he was 18. He kept his place in the team and was named as Barnsley's Young Player of the Year at the end of the season. In August 2015 he stepped up into the Premier League with Everton and made his first team debut against Tottenham on the first day of the 2016/17 campaign.

GOODISON PARK TIMELINE

1892 Goodison Park is the first major football stadium built in England, opening on 24 August 1892.

1907 The stadium starts to really take shape when a double-decker stand is built at the Park End.

1909 A second tier is added to the Main Stand.

1910 Goodison hosts the FA Cup final replay between Newcastle United and Barnsley.

1926 The next big change as another double-decker is built on the Bullens Road side. Archibald Leitch is again the architect, including the famous blue and white 'criss-cross' in the design.

1938 Goodison is now the only ground in Britain to have four double-decker stands after the re-improvement to the Gwladys Street end.

1948 Goodison's record attendance, 78,299, sees a Merseyside derby against Liverpool.

1957 The new floodlights at Goodison are switched on for the very first time.

1966 Goodison stages five games during the World Cup, including the semi-final between West Germany and Russia.

1994 The new Stanley Park End stand is built.

QUIZ: LEGENDS V THE BLUES

This will test your footy knowledge! Here are twelve Premier League legends in action over the years against Everton. All you have to do is name them all... but be careful, some of them are pictured in their younger days!

Answers on p.60-61

1

2

3

4
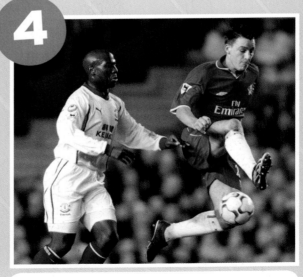

5

6

7

8

9

10

HAT-TRICK HEROES

It's every Evertonian's dream to wear the royal blue jersey and smash home a hat-trick for the Blues! These guys did just that – in fact, unbelievably, Dixie Dean did it 37 times! Yes...THIRTY-SEVEN hat-tricks for Everton! And here's Dixie himself and six other players who have earned themselves a match-ball...

Steve Watson played most of his Everton career at full-back but in September 2003 he scored three times as the Blues defeated Leeds United 4-0. Duncan Ferguson scored the other goal.

The greatest goalscorer who ever played the game. 37 times he bagged at least three in a game and famously scored a hat-trick against Arsenal at Goodison in 1928 to reach his magical figure of 60 league goals in a single season.

Steven Naismith's hat-trick was against Chelsea in September 2013. Amazingly, the Scottish international didn't even start the game – he came on as a 9th minute substitute for the injured Mo Besic.

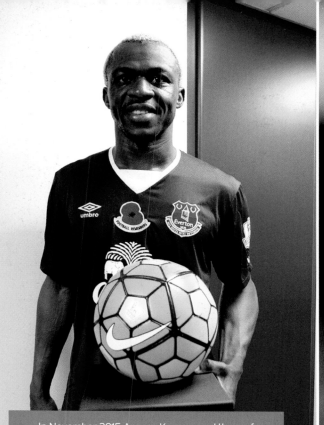

In November 2015 Arouna Kone scored three of Everton's goals as they beat Sunderland 6-2 at Goodison Park. Romelu Lukaku, Gerard Deulofeu and an own goal from Sebastian Coates completed the rout.

Kevin Campbell was still technically on loan when he scored a hat-trick in May 1999 against West Ham United. Super-Kev was our top scorer that season despite only playing eight games!

BBC Match of the Day host Gary Lineker only had one season with Everton but he scored 40 goals, including three hat-tricks against Birmingham City, Manchester City and Southampton.

Big Duncan Ferguson's one and only hat-trick for Everton came against Bolton Wanderers at Goodison Park just after Christmas 1997. Everton won 3-2 and, typically, all Duncan's goals were headers!

WORDSEARCH

How many of the players in this former Blues XI can you find in the grid below? For an extra point, match them to the country where they come from!

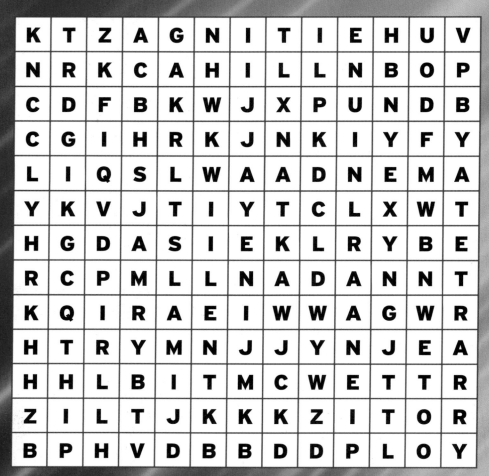

K	T	Z	A	G	N	I	T	I	E	H	U	V
N	R	K	C	A	H	I	L	L	N	B	O	P
C	D	F	B	K	W	J	X	P	U	N	D	B
C	G	I	H	R	K	J	N	K	I	Y	F	Y
L	I	Q	S	L	W	A	A	D	N	E	M	A
Y	K	V	J	T	I	Y	T	C	L	X	W	T
H	G	D	A	S	I	E	K	L	R	Y	B	E
R	C	P	M	L	L	N	A	D	A	N	N	T
K	Q	I	R	A	E	I	W	W	A	G	W	R
H	T	R	Y	M	N	J	J	Y	N	J	E	A
H	H	L	B	I	T	M	C	W	E	T	T	R
Z	I	L	T	J	K	K	K	Z	I	T	O	R
B	P	H	V	D	B	B	B	D	D	P	L	O	Y

ARTETA   AUSTRALIA

BILYALETDINOV   BELGIUM

CAHILL   CAMEROON

DISTIN   CROATIA

ETO'O   FRANCE

FELLAINI   NETHERLANDS

HEITINGA   NIGERIA

JELAVIC   RUSSIA

NAISMITH   SCOTLAND

YAKUBU   SOUTH AFRICA

PIENAAR   SPAIN

Answers on p.60-61

QUIZ: TEST A GROWN-UP!

Here's a Quiz with a difference... You are the Quiz-Master! Yes, it's YOU asking the questions. Every time an Evertonian grown-up comes around to your house, ask them these twelve questions and see who gets the most right.

1 Who did we defeat in the quarter-finals of the 1985 European Cup Winners' Cup?

2 Who was the Everton manager before Joe Royle?

3 From which club did we sign Ian Snodin?

4 Duncan Ferguson only ever scored one Everton hat-trick... who against?

5 To which club did we sell Andy Johnson in 2008?

6 For which country did Yakubu play his international football?

7 Which German goalkeeper was understudy to Tim Howard during David Moyes' time at Everton?

8 Who scored the four goals in our 1995 FA Cup semi-final win against Tottenham Hotspur?

9 Who were the opponents in David Moyes' last ever game as manager? (Clue – we lost 2-1)

10 And what about Roberto Martinez – who did we play in his first Premier League match as Everton manager?

11 In 2005/06, Everton lost in both the Champions League and the UEFA Cup – against which two teams?

12 Alan Stubbs had two spells at Everton as a player. Which two teams did he leave to join the Blues?

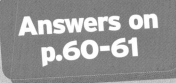

Answers on p.60-61

PLAYER PROFILES

TOM CLEVERLEY

BORN: 12 AUGUST, 1989
PLACE OF BIRTH: BASINGSTOKE, ENGLAND

Everton signed Tom in June 2015 after his contract at Manchester United expired. The energetic midfielder arrived having won a Premier League winner's medal and 13 England caps. Tom had progressed through the youth system at Old Trafford and had loan spells away with Watford, Leicester City and Wigan Athletic early in his career. A loan spell at Aston Villa in 2015 ended with an appearance in the FA Cup final at Wembley. His first goal for Everton was a last-minute winner at Newcastle on Boxing Day in 2015.

JAMES MCCARTHY

BORN: 12 NOVEMBER, 1990
PLACE OF BIRTH: GLASGOW, SCOTLAND

James has been an Everton player since the summer of 2013 when he joined from Wigan Athletic for £13million. He had previously played for Hamilton Academical in Scotland, for whom he made his debut at the age of just 15. Over the past few seasons, James has formed an effective midfield partnership with Gareth Barry. In August 2015, McCarthy pledged his long-term future to Everton by agreeing a new five-year contract and last summer he travelled to France to represent Republic of Ireland at Euro 2016.

MUHAMED BESIC

BORN: 10 SEPTEMBER, 1992
PLACE OF BIRTH: BERLIN, GERMANY

Mo arrived at Everton in the summer of 2014 after impressing for Bosnia and Herzegovina at the World Cup in Brazil, particularly against Argentina where we went up against Lionel Messi! He grew up in Germany and spent the early years of his professional career playing for Hamburg. He was signed by Everton from Hungarian team Ferencvaros and quickly became a popular player amongst fans who loved his enthusiasm, energy and fondness for a tackle. Mo underlined his commitment to the Blues by signing a new five-and-a-half year contract in March 2015.

GARETH BARRY

BORN: 23 FEBRUARY, 1981
PLACE OF BIRTH: HASTINGS, ENGLAND

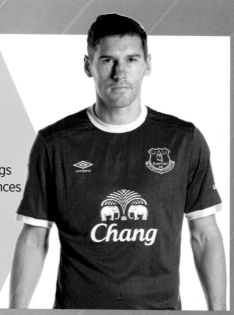

Gareth has seen and done it all in his near 20-year career at the top level. At the start of this season, only two players – Ryan Giggs and Frank Lampard – had made more Premier League appearances than the reigning Everton Player of the Season. Gareth came through the ranks at Aston Villa where he played for 12 seasons. He then moved to Manchester City where he won the FA Cup and Premier League. The 2016/17 campaign is the fourth at Goodison Park for the midfielder, who has also made 53 senior international appearances for England.

GERARD DEULOFEU

BORN: 13 MARCH, 1994
PLACE OF BIRTH: CATALONIA, SPAIN

A dazzling winger, Gerard rejoined Everton in a permanent deal from Barcelona in July 2015 – a year after a successful loan spell at Goodison Park had come to an end. It was a move that sparked much excitement among Evertonians, who fondly remembered the Spaniard's 29 appearances and four goals for the Blues during his 2013/14 stint at the Club. As a kid, Gerard joined Barcelona's La Masia academy in 2003 at the age of nine and went on to play in their first-team alongside Lionel Messi. In between his two Everton spells, Gerard had a loan spell at Sevilla with whom he won the Europa League.

ROSS BARKLEY

BORN: 5 DECEMBER, 1993
PLACE OF BIRTH: LIVERPOOL, ENGLAND

Ross is one of the shining examples of a young talented footballer to graduate through Everton's famed Academy to first-team – and international – stardom. The athletic midfielder has been with the Blues since the age of 11 and was playing for the Under-18s at 15. England international Barkley has scored some memorable goals and his return of 14 for club and country in 2015/16 was his best in a single season to date. He joined John Stones in England's 2016 Euro squad but, like his friend, he didn't get any action as the Three Lions failed to make any impact on the tournament.

QUIZ: INTERNATIONAL DOZEN...

Here are 12 players who have played for Everton in the Premier League. All you have to do is name them all... And also name the country for which they played their international football...

1

NAME

COUNTRY

2

NAME

COUNTRY

3

NAME

COUNTRY

4

NAME

COUNTRY

5

NAME

COUNTRY

6

NAME

COUNTRY

7

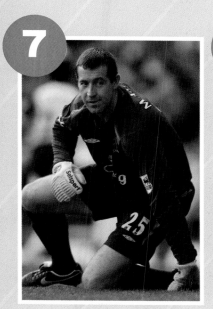

NAME

COUNTRY

8

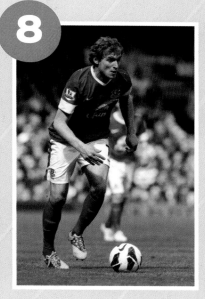

NAME

COUNTRY

9

NAME

COUNTRY

10

NAME

COUNTRY

11

NAME

COUNTRY

12

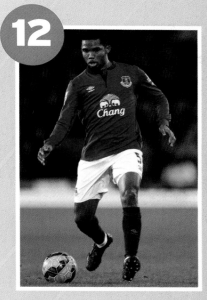

NAME

COUNTRY

Answers on p.60-61

WHEREVER THE TOFFEES GO, SO TOO DOES evertontv!

Our cameras are always rolling on match day at Goodison Park to capture all the action on the pitch - and all the excitement off it.

From the touchline to the FanZone, every angle is covered.

And if you're lucky enough to be interviewed outside the ground before kick-off, you could see yourself on the big screens inside the stadium!

evertontv also film regularly at Finch Farm - bringing you the best goals scored in training, funny features with the players, exclusive interviews and more.

If any of the squad pay a visit to a school, hospital or to surprise an unsuspecting fan, you can be sure evertontv will be there to capture it all.

The cameras also follow the Toffees on away games to guarantee Blues who can't make the journey still get to see the highlights and what was said after the final whistle.

EVER WONDERED WHAT A CAMERAMAN'S JOB INVOLVES? HEAD TO EVERTONFC.COM/EVERTONTV TO CHECK OUT ALL OF THIS CONTENT AND MORE FOR FREE!

evertonfc.com

Have you checked out the official Everton website yet?

Regular visitors to evertonfc.com know that it's the only place to get all of your news, views and all things Blues!

From the breaking news announcements directly from the Club and exclusive interviews with the manager and players, to regular features offering insight into goings-on at Goodison and Finch Farm.

The manager's pre-match press conferences can be viewed 'live' each week, as can highlights of every game over the season – usually within hours of the final whistle.

There's the odd video of players showcasing their skills, behind-the-scenes clips from the training ground and, of course, the evertontv cameras also follow the Blues on tour!

Also on the site are daily round-ups of transfer speculation where the media link the Club to players across the globe, and we bring you free apps and downloads, plus profiles of every person to have ever worn the royal blue jersey.

Interested in the young talent at Finch Farm? Learn all about the Academy, its famous graduates and current prospects – and if you're a young footballer yourself, why not join an Everton in the Community soccer camp via the website?

evertonfc.com is also your one-stop shop for all things Blue – fans can buy official merchandise, match tickets and book a stadium tour and if you want to learn about Everton's greatest moments and most unusual stories, check out the very popular interactive History Timeline. If it's about Everton Football Club…it's on evertonfc.com!

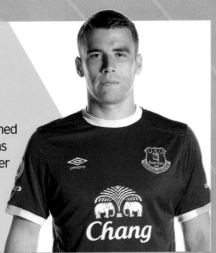

SEAMUS COLEMAN

BORN: 11 OCTOBER, 1988
PLACE OF BIRTH: KILLYBEGS, IRELAND

Republic of Ireland international Seamus Coleman is Everton's established right-back. He has been with the Club since January 2009 when he was recruited from Sligo Rovers for £60,000, having earlier begun his career at amateur team St Catherine's FC. A defender with an eye for goal, Seamus has now gone on to play over 200 matches for the Blues. At Euro 2016, he played in Ireland's four matches during the tournament and captained the team against Italy and France.

TOM DAVIES

BORN: 30 JUNE, 1998
PLACE OF BIRTH: LIVERPOOL, ENGLAND

Davies was born in Liverpool in 1998 and joined the Everton Academy at the age of just nine! He progressed very well through the youth teams at Finch Farm and signed his first professional contract in 2015. Davies made his first-team debut as a substitute at Goodison against Southampton in April 2016 and then made his first start in the last game of the season, winning the Man of the Match award. He was the captain of the England team at the 2015 FIFA Under-17 World Cup in Chile.

RAMIRO FUNES MORI

BORN: 1 JULY, 1991
PLACE OF BIRTH: MENDOZA, ARGENTINA

Ramiro moved to Goodison Park in August 2015, joining Everton from Argentine giants River Plate on a five-year contract. He contributed with important goals in his first season, including a memorable strike against Manchester City in the Capital One Cup semi-final first leg at Goodison. His form for Everton resulted in opportunities with the Argentina national side and he spent the summer of 2016 playing in the Copa America. He says enjoys training with Argentina when he has to mark Sergio Aguero and Lionel Messi...but we don't think he's telling the truth!!

ENNER VALENCIA

BORN: 4 NOVEMBER, 1989
PLACE OF BIRTH: SAN LORENZO, ECUADOR

Valencia joined Everton with about an hour left of the 2016 summer transfer window, arriving from West Ham United for an initial season-long loan. He was born in San Lorenzo in Ecuador and has represented his country more than 20 times, including the 2014 World Cup. He started his career at Emelec FC in Ecuador and then moved to Pachuca in Mexico. In 2014 he signed for West Ham for a fee estimated to be £12million. He settled very well into English football and will be determined to make an impact at Goodison.

YANNICK BOLASIE

BORN: 24 MAY, 1989
PLACE OF BIRTH: LYON, FRANCE

Bolasie's journey to Goodison Park is an unusual one! He started out in non-league football with Hillingdon Borough and then moved to the Maltese League to play for Floriana in 2007. He stayed there one season and then returned to England with Plymouth Argyle. After spells at Barnet (on loan) and Bristol City he joined Crystal Palace in 2012 and his career really took off. He became the first Palace player to score a Premier League hat-trick and he made his international debut for DR Congo. He joined Everton in 2016.

AROUNA KONE

BORN: 11 NOVEMBER, 1983
PLACE OF BIRTH: ANYAMA, IVORY COAST

Kone is an Ivory Coast international who joined Everton from Wigan Athletic in the summer of 2013 after helping the Latics to win the FA Cup. He brought with him a wealth of experience having previously played for Lierse (Belgium), Roda and PSV Eindhoven (Holland), Sevilla (Spain) and Hannover (Germany). It was whilst at PSV that he first played for Ronald Koeman! Kone arrived in English football in 2012 and played all 90 minutes for Wigan in the FA Cup final at the end of the season.

KIERAN DOWELL

BORN: 10 OCTOBER, 1997
PLACE OF BIRTH: ORMSKIRK, ENGLAND

Kieran was rewarded for an outstanding year of progress in June 2016 with a new three-year contract. The announcement came two months after the Ormskirk-born Academy graduate made his Premier League debut in a 2-1 win over Bournemouth and five weeks after his first full start in the 3-0 defeat of Norwich City. Dowell got his chance to represent the first team after a superb campaign for the Under-21s which was littered with outstanding goals. He scored 11 times for David Unsworth's men which included an audacious 40-yard chip against Southampton and a hat-trick against Leicester City – all from outside the box

PREDICTIONS

Be honest... Who predicted that Leicester City would win the Premier League last season? Nobody!!! Can they do it again?

See how well your footy crystal ball is working by trying to predict the winners of the big competitions this time around. Who'll win the FA Cup; who will conquer Europe? Who will score more goals than the rest in the Premier League? Why not challenge your friends to make some predictions and then see who got the most right at the end of the season!

COMPETITION	2015/16 WINNERS	2016/17 WINNERS
Premier League	Leicester City	
Championship	Burnley	
League One	Wigan Athletic	
League Two	Northampton	
Champions League	Real Madrid	
Europa League	Sevilla	
FA Cup	Manchester United	
League Cup	Manchester City	
Premier League top scorer	Harry Kane	

SPOT THE DIFFERENCE

See if you can spot the six differences between these two Everton action shots.

EURO 2016 ROUND-UP

Seven Everton players made the trip across the channel for last summer's European Championship in France. As expected, there were highs and lows for each of the Blues involved and their nations...

REPUBLIC OF IRELAND

Everton's Irish trio Seamus Coleman, James McCarthy and Aiden McGeady played a huge part as the Boys in Green reached the last 16 of a European Championship for the first time in their history. Coleman, who wore the captain's armband for a number of the games, and McCarthy both started all four games, while McGeady came off the bench in three of the encounters.

The best moment for manager Martin O'Neill and his side came in their final group game against Italy. After drawing 1-1 with Sweden and losing 3-0 to Belgium, the Republic knew only a win would be enough to progress from Group A – and they left it late as McGeady found Wes Hoolahan, who crossed for Robbie Brady to nod home an unforgettable late header. The end of the road eventually came against hosts France, who battled back from a goal down to secure their place in the quarter-finals.

But even that wasn't enough to dampen the Republic's spirits, and Coleman felt the full pride of his nation with an incredible hero's welcome as he returned to his hometown of Killybegs. Click the QR code here to watch the full-back's homecoming!

BELGIUM

Euro 2016 was a rollercoaster ride that eventually ended in disappointment for Romelu Lukaku and Belgium.

The Blues striker starred in the Red Devils' clash with Republic of Ireland, scoring two goals in a 3-0 victory as his nation went through to the knockout stages.

But Marc Wilmots' side, who were dubbed the 'Golden Generation' of Belgian football, fell in their last-16 clash with Wales – the tournament's surprise package.

ENGLAND

It was frustration all round for the Toffees' English contingent. The Three Lions scraped through the group stages before being eliminated by underdogs Iceland in the last 16. Both Ross Barkley and John Stones were unused substitutes for all four of England's games.

SWITZERLAND

After making his senior international debut in late March, Shani Tarashaj's brilliant performances for club and country convinced manager Vladimir Petkovic to include him in Switzerland's final 23-man squad for the summer tournament.

And the Blues' January signing, who was the fourth youngest member of the group at the age of 21, made it on the pitch as a late substitute in the Swiss' second match, a 1-1 draw with Romania.

PENALTY SHOOT-OUT

Here are some photographs of Everton penalty kicks. The spot is 12 yards from the goal line and it's just the kicker against the goalie... All you have to do is decide whether or not the ball ended up in the back of the net!

1

☐ GOAL   ☐ MISS

2

3

☐ GOAL   ☐ MISS   ☐ GOAL   ☐ MISS

4

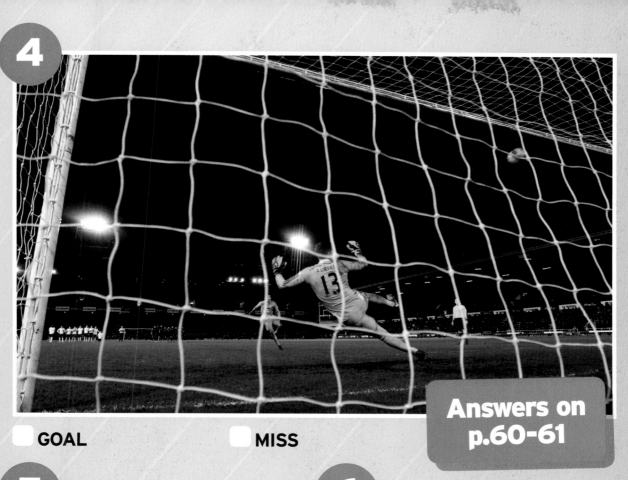

☐ GOAL   ☐ MISS

Answers on p.60-61

5

☐ GOAL   ☐ MISS

6

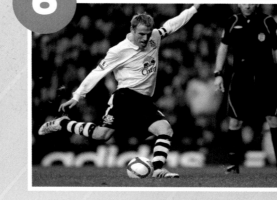

☐ GOAL   ☐ MISS

7

☐ GOAL   ☐ MISS

8

☐ GOAL   ☐ MISS

EVERTON SUPPORTERS' CLUBS

"IT'S A GRAND OLD TEAM TO SUPPORT..."

We are proud to have more than 135 Supporters' Clubs in countries across the world, including the United Kingdom, Thailand, Australia, Canada, Ireland, South Africa, India and USA.

So, whether you can see Goodison Park from your bedroom window or you live on the opposite side of the globe, we have all bases covered!

These Clubs offer fans a range of exclusive benefits, allowing you to get closer to Everton than ever before.

Joining a supporters' club is a great way to make new friends, as well as helping your chances of getting tickets to go and watch the Toffees in action.

There is also a special End of Season Awards evening, with Supporters' Clubs given the opportunity to recognise the best performers during the campaign.

To find out if there is an affiliated Everton Supporters' Club in your area, visit evertonfc.com/supportersclubs.

If there is, you will also find information about how to contact the relevant Supporters' Club secretary.

But remember, you must ask permission from your parent or guardian before making any calls or signing up to one of our clubs!

MY YEAR...
LEIGHTON BAINES

Everton's England international defender Leighton Baines is so much more than just a footballer. He is the perfect ambassador for Everton Football Club and is always one of the first players to volunteer whenever we need someone to make a charitable or personal appearance. This is a taste of what Bainesy was up to during the 2016/17 season...

While he was out injured, Leighton popped into the Matchday Hub Centre by the stadium to meet the fans.

Just before Christmas, he visited a local school to pass out some Christmas cards — and he didn't even mind wearing a Christmas jumper!

Every year, Everton Football Club puts smiles on the faces of young children who are perhaps not as fortunate as others and who else but Leighton offered to drop some gifts off.

Young people love to ask professional footballers questions about their lives and their careers and Leighton was in the hot-seat when he visited a Merseyside college.

The famous Alder Hey Children's Hospital treats thousands of young people every year and Leighton is a proud patron — even visiting when he was on crutches!

When a young Evertonian won a prize to visit a toy shop, Leighton was quick to offer to push the trolley!

Every Premier League team has its own Reading Star — a player who encourages children to read more books. Guess who our Reading Star is...!

In between all his commitments off the pitch, Leighton found time to play football for Everton!!

Leighton is seen here being mic'd up for an appearance on the Everton TV Show. He was very good too! He may be on Match of the Day one day!

Goodison Park staged a junior Premier League tournament at the end of the season and Leighton took time out to present the medals. What a busy year!

Would you like Leighton Baines to call into your class this season? Of course you would! To be in with a chance of getting our left-back into your school, simply answer this question: From which team did Everton sign Leighton Baines?

Email your answer to annual@evertonfc.com and one lucky reader will be getting a classroom visit from a Premier League footballer!

EVERTON VICTORIOUS!

The story of how the Blues lifted the Dallas Cup!

In 2016, Everton Under-18s conquered America!

The young Blues made the long trip to the United States in March and when they returned home just under two weeks later, the Dallas Cup was coming back with them!

The Dallas Cup is one of the most prestigious youth competitions in football and Everton's talented group of teenagers put the Club's name on the trophy after beating teams from all over the world.

In the space of eight days, the Under-18s played five matches, sealing glory with a victory over English rivals Fulham in the final.

It was a busy schedule that started with a match against Mexican side Tigres at the enormous 90,000 capacity Cotton Bowl Stadium. It ended with an unlucky 1-0 defeat – but it gave the Everton players more motivation to march on and win the competition.

The next day, the young Toffees were handed the task of facing Japanese side Kyoto Sanga, this time at the much smaller venue of Richland College. Nathan Broadhead's penalty and Delial Brewster's fine individual goal earned a 2-1 win and kept Everton's Dallas Cup hopes alive!

It was back to the Cotton Bowl for the third group game against Real Salt Lake – and it was another victory for Kevin Sheedy's youngsters. The same two players who scored against Kyoto Sanga – Brewster and Broadhead – again hit the net, as did central defender Callum Lees. A 3-1 triumph meant that Everton were into the semi-finals.

Next up it was hosts FC Dallas, with the game taking place at MLS ground Toyota Stadium. Everton were in control when Jack Kiersey bundled the ball over the line midway through the first half, and Brewster and Broadhead then each got their third goals of the tournament to put the seal on another impressive 3-1 win!

Who is Delial Brewster?

Delial was Everton's hero at the Dallas Cup, scoring five goals during the tournament, including two in the final.

The striker originally comes from Southport and has been with Everton's Academy since he was 12-years-old.

Delial is left-footed and last season he went out to play on loan at Stockport, scoring just 15 minutes into his debut against Nuneaton Borough!

And Sunday 27 March was a night to remember for Everton's Under-18s players, who got their hands on winners' medals by beating Fulham 2-1 in the final. Brewster ensured he also picked up the Player of the Tournament award by scoring both goals. Great scenes of delight followed as the players and staff revelled in the glory – with coach Kevin Sheedy even getting soaked with water!

Then it was the long flight back home to Merseyside. The players were again able to celebrate the great achievement on the final day of the 2015/16 Premier League season when they were invited onto the Goodison Park pitch at half-time against Norwich City to show the trophy off to almost 40,000 Evertonians!

Where is Dallas?

Dallas is a city in Texas, located in the heart of the United States, which is a 10-hour flight from England. The area is famous for its cowboys and, indeed, the city's American football team is named after them.

Everton defender Ramiro Funes Mori spent time living in Dallas when he was a teenager – that's why he speaks such good English!

Dallas is also the place where President JFK was infamously shot and killed in 1963.

QUIZ ANSWERS

PAGE 13
TONY'S QUICK QUIZ
1. Stoke City
2. Swansea City
3. Ipswich Town
4. Charlton Athletic
5. Bournemouth
6. Portsmouth
7. Burnley
8. Middlesbrough

PAGE 16
QUIZ: AGAINST THE BLUES
1. Gareth Barry, Aston Villa
2. Yannick Bolasie, Crystal Palace
3. Tom Cleverley, Wigan Athletic
4. Idrissa Gueye, RSC Lille
5. Ashley Williams, Swansea City
6. Aaron Lennon, Tottenham Hotspur
7. James McCarthy, Wigan Athletic

PAGE 17
QUIZ: AND IF YOU KNOW YOUR HISTORY
1. Seamus Coleman (✓) v Mikel Arteta
2. Ross Barkley v Kevin Campbell (✓)
3. Gareth Barry (✓) v Nigel Martyn
4. Phil Jagielka v David Unsworth (✓)
5. James McCarthy v Marouane Fellaini (✓)
6. Leighton Baines (✓) v Duncan Ferguson

PAGE 49 SPOT THE DIFFERENCE

PAGE 24
QUIZ: THE LOCAL LADS
1. D - Dan Gosling
2. AEK Athens
3. True - Wayne Rooney
4. D - Manchester City
5. C - James Vaughan
6. B - FC Krasnodar

PAGE 25
QUIZ: IF YOU KNOW YOUR HISTORY...
1. C - Dixie Dean
2. D - Nine
3. D - Dave Watson
4. True
5. C - 40
6. B - Howard Kendall

PAGE 34-35
QUIZ: LEGENDS V THE BLUES!
1. Ryan Giggs
2. Alan Shearer
3. Peter Schmeichel
4. John Terry
5. Roy Keane
6. Denis Bergkamp
7. Frank Lampard
8. Thierry Henry
9. Gianfranco Zola
10. Paulo Di Canio
11. Paul Scholes
12. Teddy Sheringham

PAGE 39
QUIZ: TEST A GROWN-UP!
1. Fortuna Sittard
2. Mike Walker
3. Leeds United
4. Bolton Wanderers
5. Fulham
6. Nigeria
7. Steffan Wessels
8. Daniel Amokachi (2), Graham Stuart and Matt Jackson
9. Chelsea, away
10. Norwich City, away
11. Villarreal and Dynamo Bucharest
12. Celtic and Sunderland

PAGE 42-43
QUIZ: INTERNATIONAL DOZEN...
1. Andy van der Meyde; Holland
2. Jo; Brazil
3. John Heitinga; Holland
4. Joleon Lescott; England
5. Landon Donovan; USA
6. Mark Hughes; Wales
7. Nigel Martyn; England
8. Nikica Jelavic; Croatia
9. Paul Gascoigne; England
10. Phil Neville; England
11. Richard Gough; Scotland
12. Samuel Eto'o; Cameroon

PAGE 52
PENALTY SHOOT-OUT
1. GOAL
2. GOAL
3. MISS
4. MISS
5. MISS
6. GOAL
7. MISS
8. GOAL

PAGE 38 WORDSEARCH

K	T	Z	A	G	N	I	T	I	E	H	U	V
N	R	K	C	A	H	I	L	L	N	B	O	P
C	D	F	B	K	W	J	X	P	U	N	D	B
C	G	I	H	R	K	J	N	K	I	Y	F	Y
L	I	Q	S	L	W	A	A	D	N	E	M	A
Y	K	V	J	T	I	Y	T	C	L	X	W	T
H	G	D	A	S	I	E	K	L	R	Y	B	E
R	C	P	M	L	L	N	A	D	A	N	N	T
K	Q	I	R	A	E	I	W	W	A	G	W	R
H	T	R	Y	M	N	J	J	Y	N	J	E	A
H	H	L	B	I	T	M	C	W	E	T	T	R
Z	I	L	T	J	K	K	K	Z	I	T	O	R
B	P	H	V	D	B	B	B	D	D	P	L	O	Y